MW00992637
RIGIDLY ANCHORED
30
I wonder if you've ever
Willow sheltering a hyen
Nowhere in nature can be found
An opposition more profound:
A sad tree weeping inconsolably!
A wild beast laughing uncontrollably!
What's best is to have is just enough;
But knowing what that is is tough.
WARDS RIVERSIDE
AIR CUSHION
HAND
50 Click
5D33
D
T
May 19, 1994
Henrik Drescher
Via Facsimile
Dear Henrik:
I am amazed and delighted--at the art, first of
and secondly, at the spelling. Both are very, ve
good and I have only a few small corrections, only
of which will cause, I think, grief. That one is on
the making faces page where you left out a word. The
line "and rolling both eyes about" should read "and
rolling both your eyes about." I hope it can be fixed,
because I am much more rigid than Dick about the manu-
script. Is there a comma after "stuck out" in the
3rd line? It's not quite clear on the xerox. There
should be.
That's the worst news
The Opposite of Pi
line 9.
The mirror is perf
Stop and Go. Shou
having "Bye" on bot
on the other? "Far
The Opposite of Bal

RUNAWAY OPPOSITES

POEMS BY RICHARD WILBUR • PICTURES BY HENRIK DRESCHER

HARCOURT BRACE & COMPANY
SAN DIEGO, NEW YORK, LONDON • PRINTED IN SINGAPORE

DF2
J811.52
W
C.1

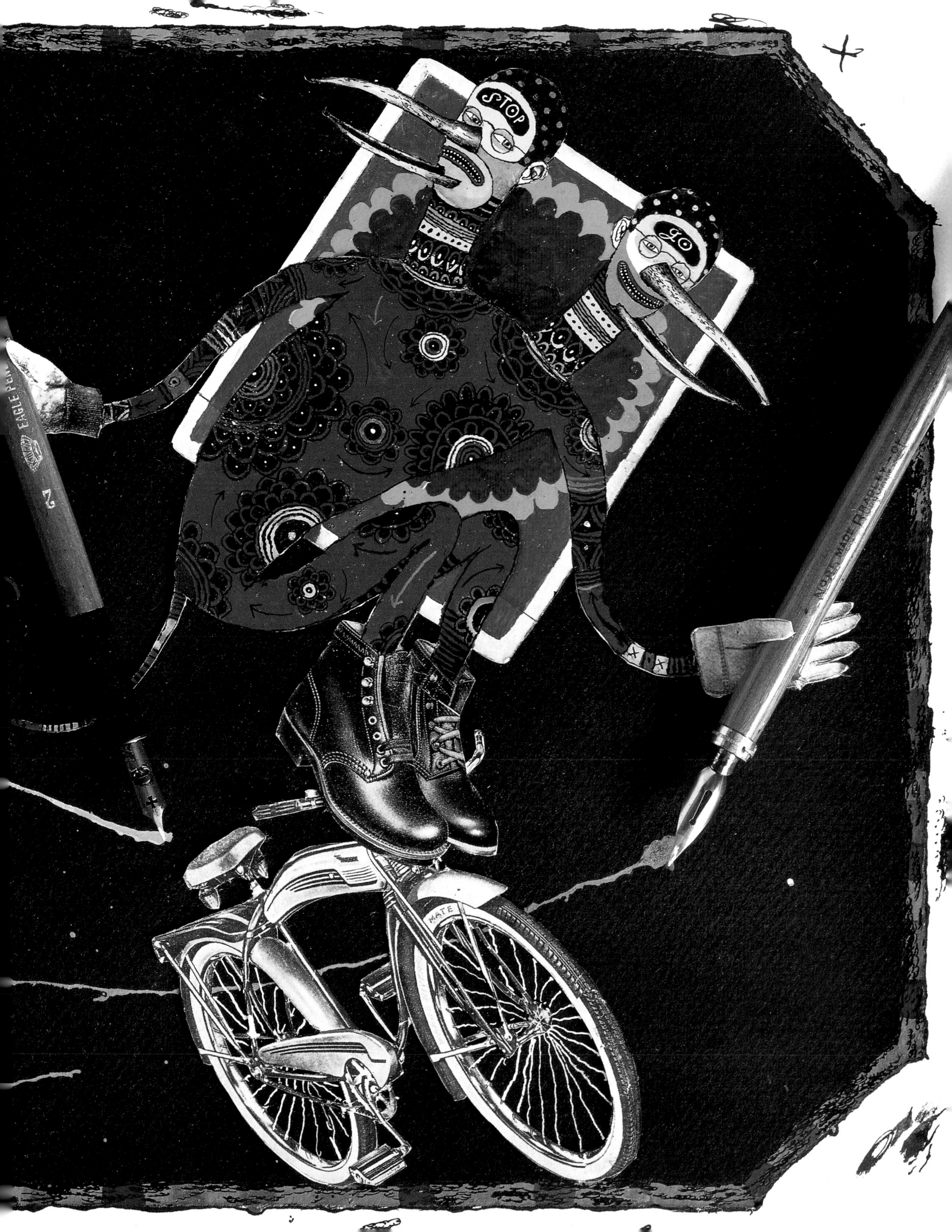
STOP
GO
MATE

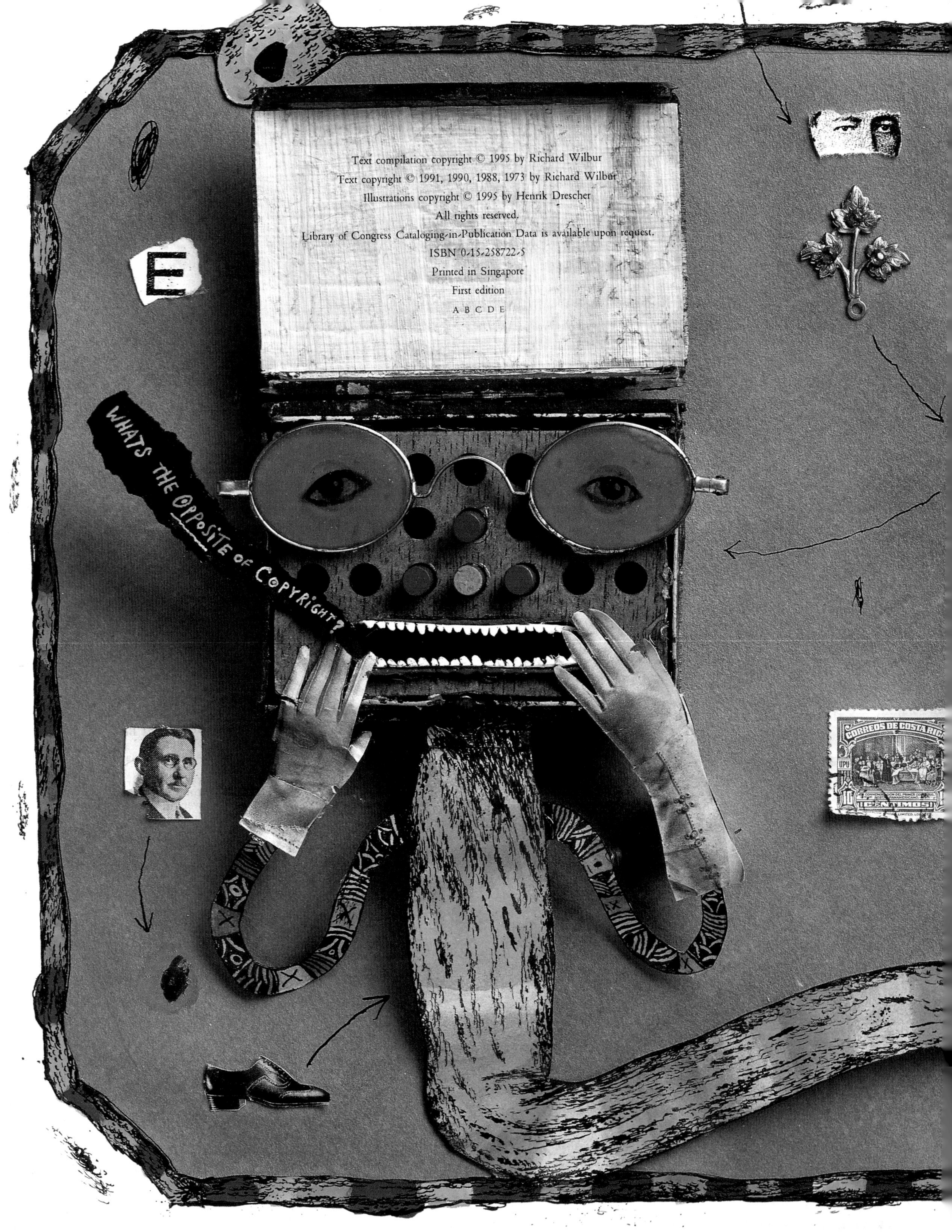
Text compilation copyright © 1995 by Richard Wilbur
Text copyright © 1991, 1990, 1988, 1973 by Richard Wilbur
Illustrations copyright © 1995 by Henrik Drescher
All rights reserved.
Library of Congress Cataloging-in-Publication Data is available upon request.
ISBN 0-15-258722-5
Printed in Singapore
First edition
A B C D E

FOR VALERIE, BOB, EMMA, LUC, AND BOUGE → H.D.
FOR GABRIEL, AMELIA, AND LIAM → R.W.
McMillan, Ferndale.
CANADA
0700
T
O
H

WHAT IS THE OPPOSITE OF NUTS?
IT'S SOUP! LET'S HAVE NO IFS OR BUTS.
IN ANY SUITABLE REPAST
THE SOUP COMES FIRST, THE NUTS COME LAST.
OR THAT IS WHAT SANE FOLKS ADVISE;
YOU'RE NUTS IF YOU THINK OTHERWISE.
NUT SOUP
SCREW LOOSE

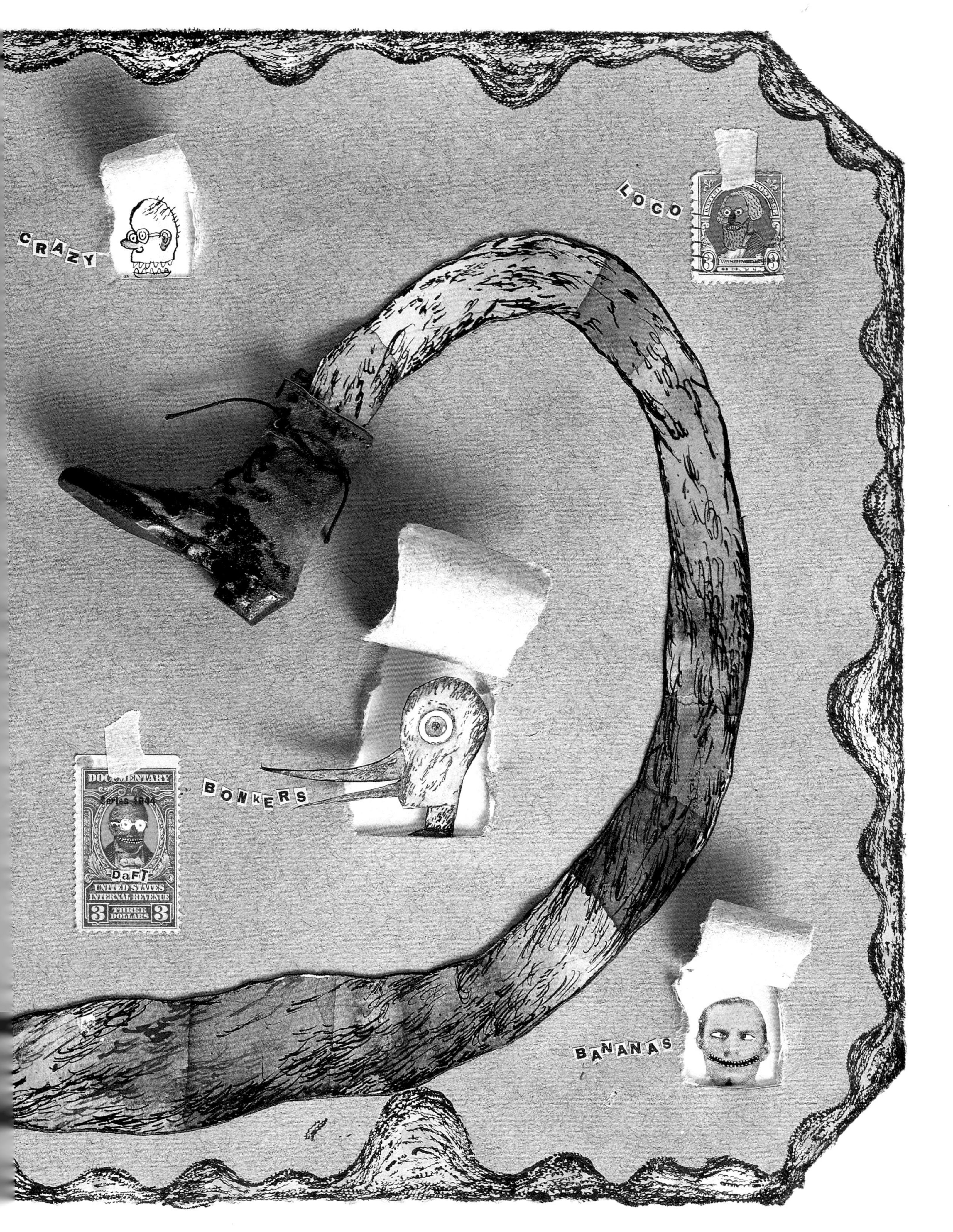
CRAZY
LOCO
DOCUMENTARY
Series 1944
BONKERS
DaFT
UNITED STATES
INTERNAL REVENUE
3 THREE DOLLARS 3
BANANAS

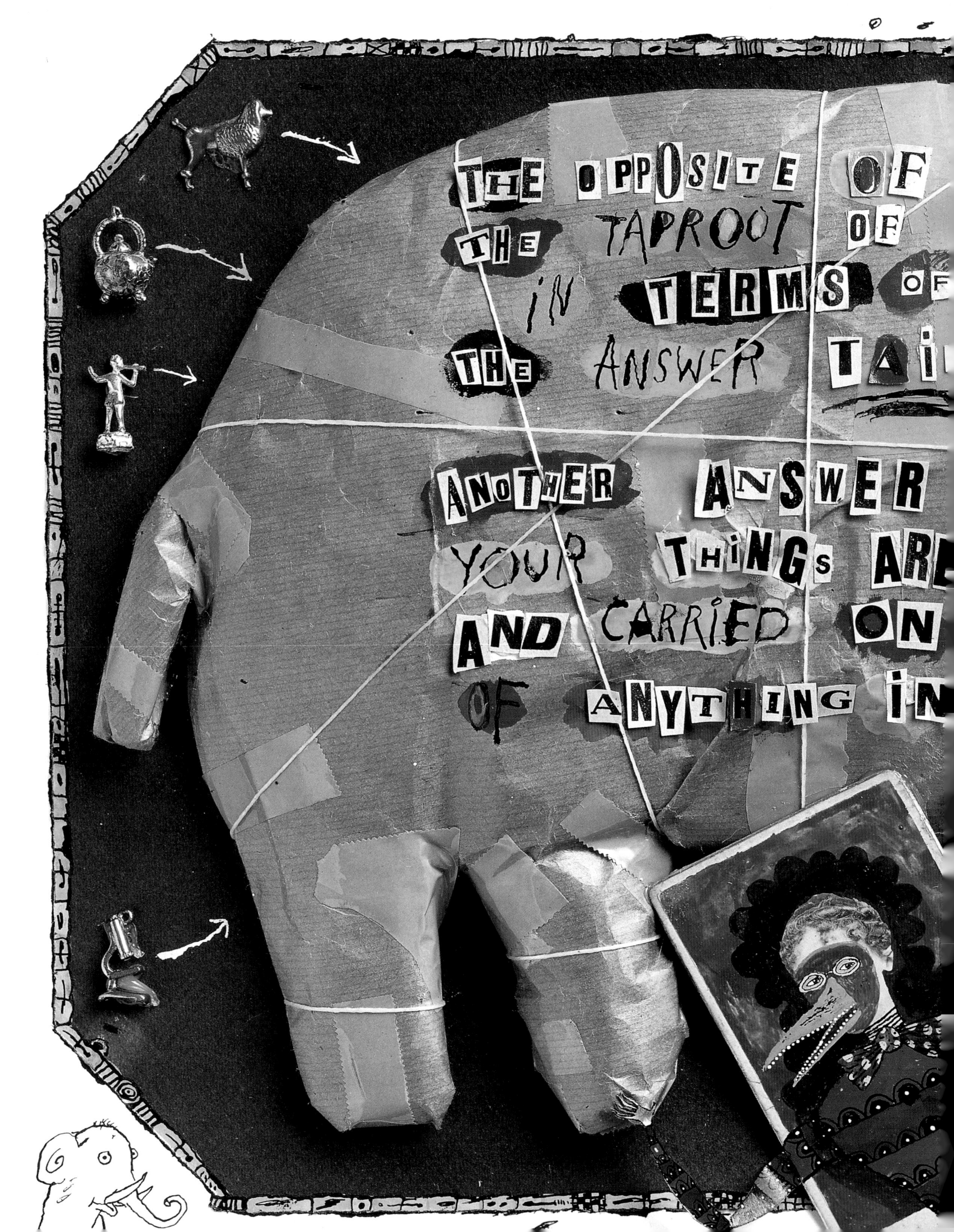
THE OPPOSITE OF
THE TAPROOT OF
IN TERMS OF
THE ANSWER TA
ANOTHER ANSWER
YOUR THINGS AR
AND CARRIED ON
OF ANYTHING IN

TRUNK COULD BE
A CEDAR TREE.
ELEPHANTS, HOWEVER,
IS RATHER CLEVER.
IS WHEN ALL
TIED UP IN A BALL
YOUR HEAD, FOR LACK
WHICH TO PACK.

THE OPPOSITE OF ROBBER? COME,
YOU KNOW THE ANSWER. DON'T BE DUMB!
WHILE ROBBERS TAKE THINGS FOR A LIVING,
PHILANTHROPISTS ARE FOND OF GIVING.
"AND YET," YOU SAY, "THAT'S NOT QUITE TRUE.
PHILANTHROPISTS ARE TAKERS, TOO,
AND OFTEN HAVE BEEN VERY GREEDY
BEFORE THEY THOUGHT TO HELP THE NEEDY."
WELL, LET'S BE OBVIOUS, THEN: THE OP

OSITE OF ROBBER IS A COP.

A MIDDLE,
WHICH YOU
WOULD BE WISE
TO CLOTHE AS WELL,
OR YOU'LL BE
CHILLY
AND RUN THE
RISK OF LOOKING
Silly.

WHAT IS THE OPPOSITE OF

HAT?

IT ISN'T HARD TO ANSWER THAT.

IT'S SHOES,

FOR SHOES AND HAT TOGETHER

PROTECT OUR TWO EXTREMES FROM WEATHER.

BETWEEN THESE TWO EXTREMES

YO! THAT WRITING LOOKS LIKE CHINESE FROM THIS ANGLE.

DR. WALTERS
CHILL CURE
A POWERFUL MALARIA GERM KILLER
SEROCO CHEMICAL LABORATORY
CHICAGO
THE OPPOSITE OF
THAT'S NOT SO VERY
A DOCTOR'S NICE
HE MAKES YOU
THEN WHAT'S HIS OPPOSITE
IT'S ANYONE WHO
SEROCO
LITHIA
TABLETS
CONTAINING
3 GRAINS CITRATE
LITHIA
SEROCO CHEMICAL
LABORATORY
CHICAGO
ILLINOIS
DR.
HAMMOND'S
SYRUP
HYPOPHOSPHITES
COMPOUND
PETROLEUM
JELLY

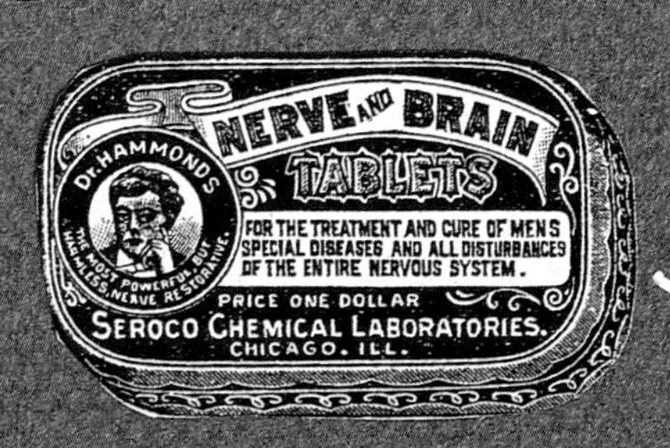

DR. HAMMOND'S
NERVE AND BRAIN TABLETS
FOR THE TREATMENT AND CURE OF MEN'S SPECIAL DISEASES AND ALL DISTURBANCES OF THE ENTIRE NERVOUS SYSTEM.
PRICE ONE DOLLAR
SEROCO CHEMICAL LABORATORIES.
CHICAGO, ILL.

DOCTOR? WELL,

HARD TO TELL.

ND WHEN YOU'RE ILL

BETTER WITH A PILL.

ON'T BE THICK!

MAKES YOU SICK.

OLD ENGLISH WART REMOVER

I wonder if you've ever seen a
willow sheltering a hyena?
Nowhere in nature can be found
an opposition more profound:
a sad tree weeping inconsolably!
a wild beast laughing uncontrollably

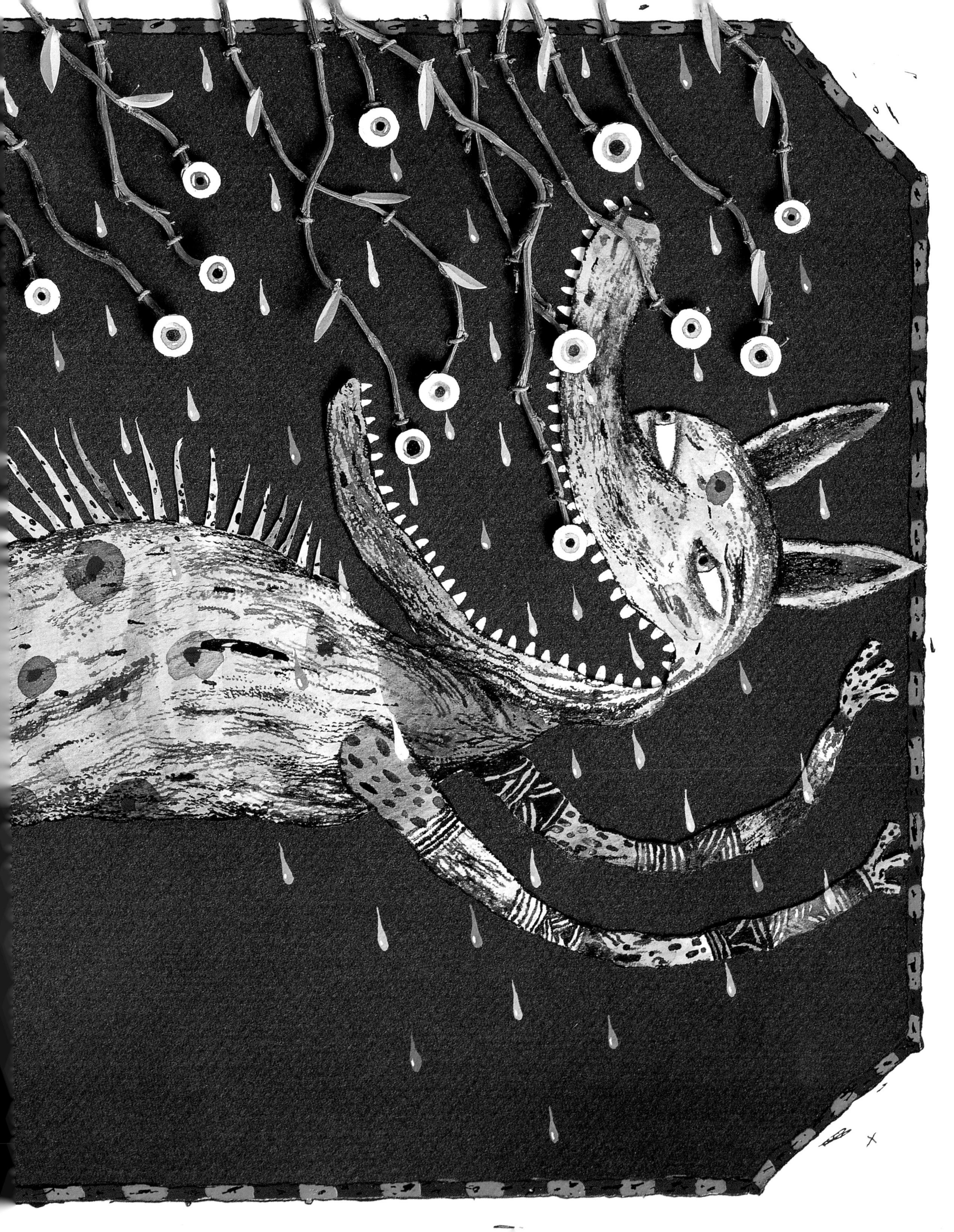

THE OPPOSITE OF STANDING STILL IS WALKING UP OR DOWN A HILL
STANDING
STILL

RUNNING BACKWARDS, CREEPING, CRAWLING,
LEAPING OFF A CLIFF
AND FALLING,
Turning SOMERSAULTS IN GRAVEL,
OR ANY OTHER MODE OF TRAVEL.

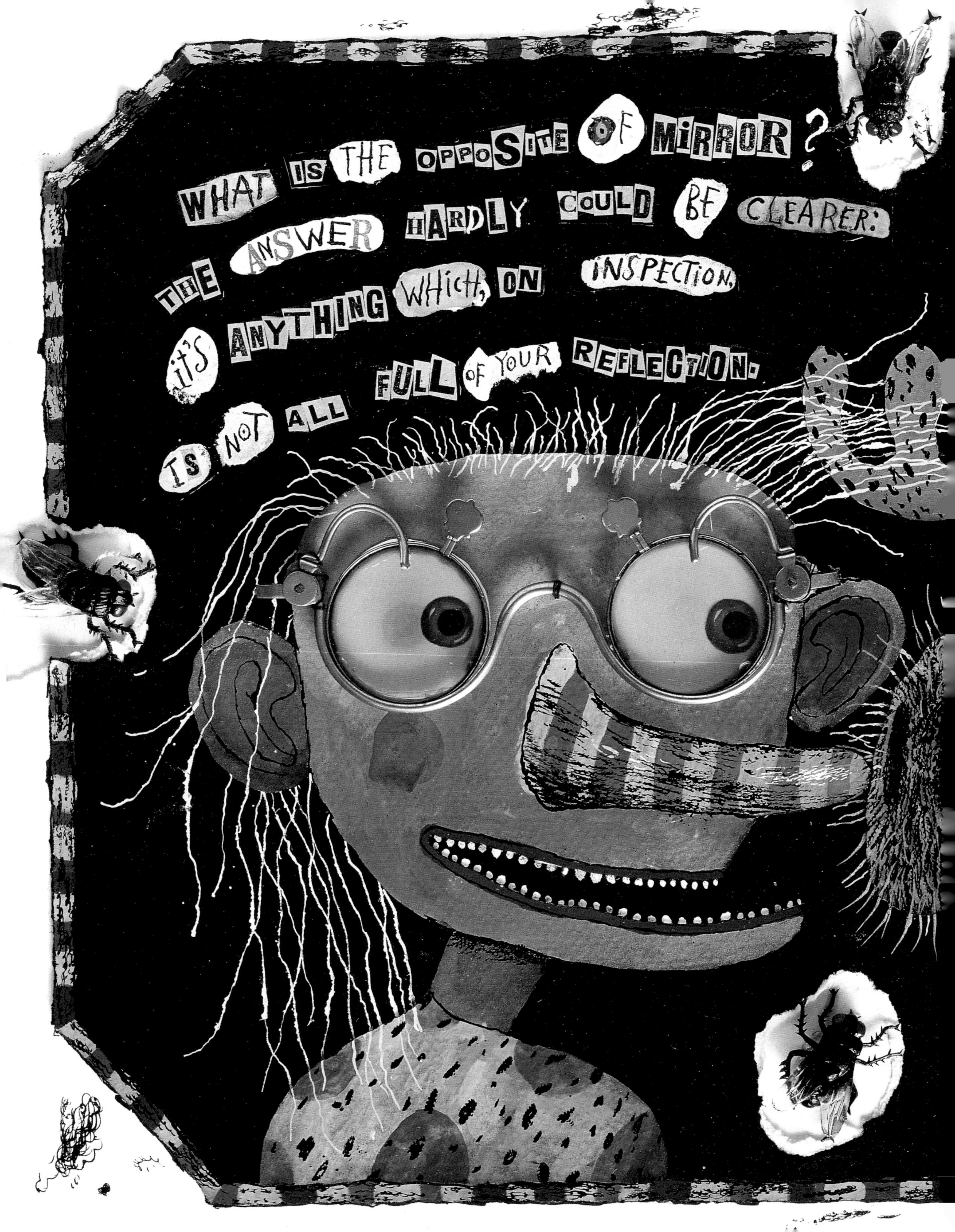
WHAT IS THE OPPOSITE OF MIRROR?
THE ANSWER HARDLY COULD BE CLEARER:
IT'S ANYTHING WHICH, ON INSPECTION,
IS NOT ALL FULL OF YOUR REFLECTION.

FOR INSTANCE, IT WOULD BE NO USE
TO BRUSH YOUR HAIR BEFORE A MOOSE,
OR TRY A RAINCOAT ON FOR SIZE
WHILE LOOKING AT A SWARM OF FLIES.

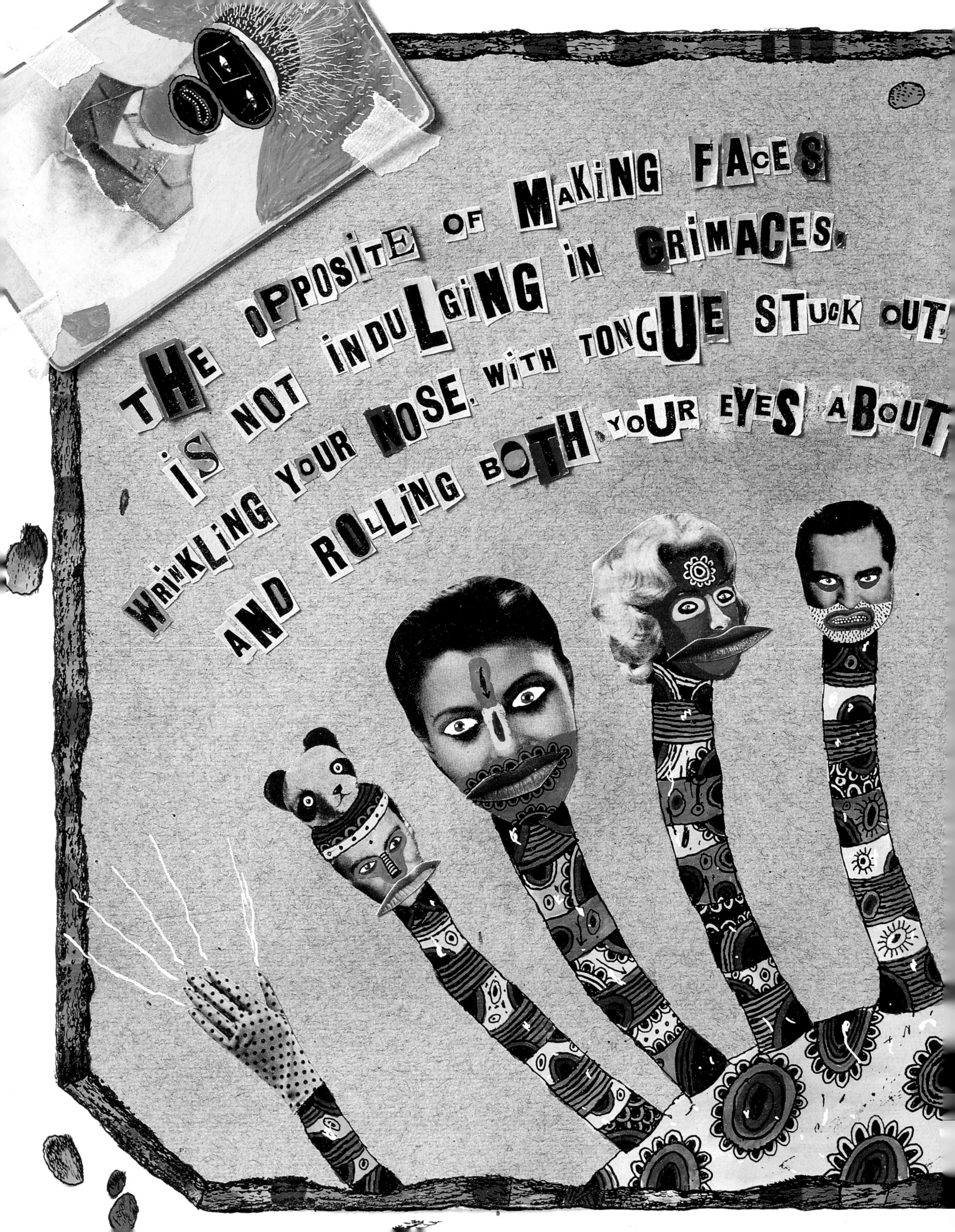
THE OPPOSITE OF MAKING FACES
IS NOT INDULGING IN GRIMACES,
WRINKLING YOUR NOSE, WITH TONGUE STUCK OUT,
AND ROLLING BOTH YOUR EYES ABOUT

BUT LETTING EYES, AND MOUTH, AND NOSE
REMAIN ENTIRELY IN REPOSE.
IT'S TRUE, HOWEVER, THAT A VERY
FIXED EXPRESSION CAN BE SCARY.

AND MERELY MAKE A DREADFUL
HOLE
HOME RUN!
A HOLE IN ONE!
SOFT-BALL
REGULATION
Official
SOFT BALL
FUSED KAPOK CENTER
Semi-Pro League

WHAT IS THE OPPOSITE OF BALL?
IT'S METEOR. THOUGH METEORS FALL
AS BALLS DO, AND LIKE BALLS ARE ROUND,
AND THOUGH THEY SOMETIMES HIT THE GROUND,
THEY DON'T KNOW HOW TO BOUNCE OR ROLL

WHAT IS THE OPPOSITE OF BABY?
THE ANSWER IS A GROWN-UP,
MAYBE.
I WANT MY MOMMY!

PYREX
TYRANNOSAURUSMOM!

WHAT IS THE OPPOSITE OF RIOT?
COCK-A-DOODLE-DOO
BOW WOW

Hush!
IT'S LOTS OF PEOPLE KEEPING QUIET.
BAA
5 CENTS 5

WHAT IS THE OPPOSITE OF PILLOW?
THE ANSWER, CHILD, IS ARMADILLO.
"OH, DON'T TALK NONSENSE!" YOU PROTEST.
HOWEVER, IF YOU TRIED TO REST
YOUR HEAD UPON THE CREATURE, YOU
WOULD FIND THAT WHAT I SAY IS TRUE.
IT ISN'T SOFT. FROM HEAD TO TAIL
IT WEARS A SCRATCHY COAT OF MAIL.
AND FURTHERMORE, IT WON'T HOLD STILL
UPON A BED, AS PILLOWS WILL,
BUT SQUIRMS, AND JUMPS AT EVERY CHANCE
TO RUN AWAY AND EAT SOME ANTS.
SO THERE! ADMIT THAT I WAS RIGHT,
OR ELSE WE'LL HAVE A PILLOW FIGHT.
Goose
Duck